The Scent of Forgotten Love

ARCHANA BHARATHI

POEMS

Made with ♥ on the Notion Press Platform
www.notionpress.com

*Where will I go for the words for my poem when
life believes it has taken love from my heart?*

*I'm deceiving life to make it feel better for a while,
because neither the love nor the words can be
taken away from me.*

*Until life realizes this delusion before its eyes,
all my love and poems are transcended
through muted words.*

CONTENTS

• • •

LONGING NESTLES

You flew like a dove
tracing no path
taking all our love.

In the noisy world,
You are the melody
I choose and yearn for…
There is no noise now
yet this quiet place
is not easing the pain
of your absence…
Your laughter echoes
in my mind;
Your scent lives
in this home
Even after the storm.

ARCHANA BHARATHI

Craving for your affection

As the flowers down
their head in the
lively evening,
I down myself
when you disappeared
in the twilight.

The soft breezes
that danced on my face
makes me crave of
Your tender touch…

This craving for your affection
is incessantly tormenting
The heart that was
Loved by you once.

ARCHANA BHARATHI

The invisible distance

Why have you dug
a deep huge crack
between us?

How could I reach you
when you stand
on the other side
wishing it to grow bigger?

Would you have some concern
when I jump into the crack
filled with silence and waiting,
only to reach you again?

I hope my longing
comes to an end
when all my tears
fill the crack until
it makes me float
to behold you...

ARCHANA BHARATHI

The daring heart
which seeks and find
Love that's true,
ceaselessly hunts
until finding a love
in a gentle rain
that washes my sin.

To find a love
which fuels my life
in the midst of uncertainty
is all I least wish for…

ARCHANA BHARATHI

This punishment of
reticent and restraining
from communication
is beyond exhausting…

The need to hear
my name from you
may become the
last wish of mine…

Realizing that
Silence is never
equal to peace!

ARCHANA BHARATHI

Where are You?

Where are your palms
that held my face
in the cold night
to warm my soul?

Where are your eyes
that searched me
just after entering
Our home after
a long tiring day?

Where is your voice
that called my name
For every little moment
from finding things
to sharing secrets?

Where are you?
Where could I
find you,
After you left saying
'Don't Search me'?

ARCHANA BHARATHI

Am I not supposed
to be around you,
though whatever happens
between us?

A Vow to be together
till the last is
still etched in me…

As long as I live,
I search for you
I come to you…
I hope our hide and seek
Stops one day, but now
Where are you?

What if you don't like me
if I find you?

ARCHANA BHARATHI

The Abstract Art

You are the pain
Which makes my life
Beautiful yet tragic.
You are the stain
On my red heart -
Abstract yet unfaded.
You are the vain
Where my efforts are
Abundant yet unrecognized…

ARCHANA BHARATHI

Cloud mail

Do the clouds

ever wish

to touch the moon?

Shall I just convey

The clouds about

My thoughts of you?

But first, Sending you

a reminder to smile.

ARCHANA BHARATHI

• • •

WILTED HOPES

Precious you

When you are mirage
To the eyes of the world;
She saw you as oasis
To her thirst of life.

ARCHANA BHARATHI

Freedom's paradox

The freedom you wish
is to wander around;
my freedom I wish
is only to walk
beside you or
be locked with you
for the rest of the life.

ARCHANA BHARATHI

I was blowing the balloon

of happiness to present you,

Your happy face looked

extra brighter;

When I was ready

to give you the bunch of joy,

The balloon shredded into pieces,

burst by the prickle of a needless needle!

The giving hand is not taken back

and it wasn't ready too...

Though the hand is empty,

the heart wishes for a magic!

The smile of us faded away in black,

the piteous is you or me?

ARCHANA BHARATHI

Unintentional ruins

Did I burn the home
Unintentionally?
Did I lose my safe place?

Every time I dwelt
In the home,
Reminds me of the
Comfort and safety
To all the vulnerability!

How will I ever
Wish to leave it?
The matchstick
In the hand is
for lighting up
to witness the
beauty of home
in furtherance…

ARCHANA BHARATHI

The bloody wind
dragged the fire
in my hand
to ignite all
that resided in
The little home…

Did I burn the home
Unintentionally?
Did I lose my safe place?
Did I tear down myself
in the midst of fire
at the home?

ARCHANA BHARATHI

A bond so deep, yet insecure

to hold too tight, to let it be –

too close for friends,

yet love feels far out

who will walk the line so thin,

where friendship fades and love begins?

If we call it love, do we lose our place?

If we stay as friends, will longing erase?

Between the poles,

A soul must choose,

to risk it all or fear to lose.

ARCHANA BHARATHI

Braving rejection

You poke my soul
with your dismissal
without even touching
in a glimpse…

You overlook the
unwavering peace
that I have in my hands
to present to you.

You opt firmly
not to have me
as part of yours…
With due respect
My pity heart
hides itself from your sight,
Yet longing to be found
By your corner eyesight at least…

ARCHANA BHARATHI

Destiny

Blessing or cursing?

Genie in the lamp or imp on the tree?

Peace or anger?

Perplexed mind or a clarified soul?

Life as tossing coin -

Resting in my hands!

Yet, the flips decided answer

Just like the destiny

contemplated us.

ARCHANA BHARATHI

Shades of Life

From drowning in the sea of chaos
To drowning in the sea of silence;
From frowning at the reality
To smiling at the reality;
From having mercy
To becoming numb;
From being crazy
To apathetic;

Time flied with all flaws;
And again - The pretty li(f)e proved itself!

ARCHANA BHARATHI

• • •

ACHE'S EMBRACE

• • •

Though we are miles apart,
whenever I close my eyes
I see you near to me
standing as guiding light
in all ups and downs.
My fear erases once
I dream of your embrace,
Realizing our love is safe here.

ARCHANA BHARATHI

In midnight thoughts

The silent screams
have not choked
me completely
till today…
The pillow that
wiped my tears
has not soaked
in deep misery
till today…
For all the screams
and the tears,
I know I have you
in midnight thoughts,
I am not alone here.

ARCHANA BHARATHI

Ripples of you

Shallow smooth puddle is I
Crazy baby boy is you…
The stone you threw into me -
Either intended or not, is
going deep down in me!
And I see the ripples created,
are reflected in your eyes...

ARCHANA BHARATHI

Rainbow

The far you are,
The more I fall;
Let me see you a little long,
Let me be with you long last;
Climbing up the ladder
To touch you,
To feel you closely –
You faded as soon as I wished
But the colourful YOU
is printed in my soul.
I love you, my rainbow.

ARCHANA BHARATHI

Finding hope in memories

I find peace
in reminiscence;
I find comfort
in solitude
with your memory;
I find hope by
Recalling you
in my memoirs
Where our past
And present meets.

ARCHANA BHARATHI

Wishing on distant stars

In the quiet of night's embrace,
under the canvas of celestial lace,
I cast my hopes upon distant stars,
where my dreams unfold.

Each twinkle whispers secrets,
Along with those stars
The unwrapped emotions,
The unuttered truths,
The unvoiced concerns,
And the silent sentiments
Compete from this earth.
We are secrets to each other…

ARCHANA BHARATHI

Who will decipher
the language
that was coded
only by us -
with no words and
signalling sounds, yet
with secret waves
of Love,
longing to be
together in
Eternity?

ARCHANA BHARATHI

Unfurling of my emotions
has made me feel light
by confessions of my soul
In the long lovely night
through the unposted letters.

Some letters bear apologies,
Regrets that stay,
Others hold promises to be fulfilled,
A future imagined; destiny willed.
Each letter a tale of love and woe,
For even unposted, they live ever.

ARCHANA BHARATHI

Aches Embrace

Aches hold me,
soft and slow,
like a whisper
only I can know.

Hot tears keep company
on cold, quiet nights,
lingering gently,
but never to wound.

ARCHANA BHARATHI

Patience unleashes time

You are near to me;
And I am far for you...
I see you from here
And some day you
reach me from there!

I see you & you see me,
But we see each other
differently from a distance!
Yet I look for your arrival
in the shores where I wait...

The clouds turn dark,
The breeze into storm,
The waves into silence,
Before the rain comes -
I need you badly
To dance with me!

ARCHANA BHARATHI

Even the soil locked
in my hourglass wants
Its freedom from me,
Since it got tired!

But the tireless heart
With unbounded love
Still looks beyond the
Shores for your arrival…

ARCHANA BHARATHI
———————

• • •

FROM ASHES, LIGHT

Bridges of Bloom

Rifts are created
to plant flowers
between the hearts
that need to be bridged.

Nothing, yet everything

Nothing is mine
Forever to have it;
Tightly to hold it;
Sadly to leave it…

Unleashing the blindfold
Before the colors
Of life fades away…

Unarming the heart
Before the coldness
Of world freezes it…

Unlocking the life
residing in me
before the lifeless time
ends with the world.

ARCHANA BHARATHI

Nothing is mine
Forever to have it;
Tightly to hold it;
Sadly to leave it…

Everything is mine
Forever to feel it;
Happily to embrace it;
Gladly to grieve it…

ARCHANA BHARATHI

Beyond Storms and Sands

Does the desert
With its dry air
eye on the
brawny cactus
to witness
the thorns or fruits?

Does the storm there
believe that those thorns
are to tear it off?

The poor cactus
neither knows the storm
nor the desert.
The poor cactus
neither cares the rain
nor needs the same,
either to grow some
Thorns or fruits.

ARCHANA BHARATHI

The thorns are outgrown
Only to be disguised!
The subtle sweet
challenging cactus
is indifferent to
the desert with its
Stormy sands and
The rare rains!

ARCHANA BHARATHI

Inhale hope

The inflicting pain
destroys my hope
and faith to love,
Yet somewhere
in the near future
Life holds the answer
for the unanswered questions…
Until then, just
BREATHE.

ARCHANA BHARATHI

To love is human

Love resides,
Love lives.
It won't fade
It will stay forever
mixed in the air;
sedimented in memories
of all the hearts
that has ever loved.

ARCHANA BHARATHI

Not everything is fair in love and war.

WARMTH REKINDLES

The revived Melody

The piano, dusted off after years;
Silent, waiting – forgotten here.
Then your hands, unhurried,
revived the song in me.

The loud sound witnessed -
The throbbing heart of piano...
Baby, It was felt –
the random plays by you
were the best tune ever!

ARCHANA BHARATHI

Winter's end

A little hope
is fed slowly
on seeing You,
My sunshine.

In the dust
a lucid glow
is sensed
because of You,My sunshine.

A small hole
is where you
creep through
to light the
antiquated house!

ARCHANA BHARATHI

A delicate heat
yet strong enough
to Warm the
Cold hearted girl
with your sunshine!

You are my sunshine
Not just in the winters;
You are my sunshine
Even in my summers.

ARCHANA BHARATHI

The honour of waiting

I walk on the streets
where you walked...
I cross the places
that you passed...
Too near yet too far!

What hide and seek
does the time play
when we are just
a few miles away?

The hopeful lights
make all this wait
Surreal and strange
yet so beautiful...

ARCHANA BHARATHI

As the moon wanes,
My patience wades
through the months;
But as the waves again
I find immense peace in
The phase of waiting...

Under the same sky
and In the same path,
I'll walk on the street
along with you,
when the hands of
Our clocks coincide...

How will i ask you
if this waiting ends,
Will you give me
the honour of waiting
and a promise to hold
until we meet again?

ARCHANA BHARATHI

Captured in time

I'm a flawed butterfly with broken wings
and you are a dying flower about to wither.
To the world - it is stunning to see
the beautiful butterfly kissing the red flower.
No one there noticed their flaws;
Instead, they captured the scene -
Little moments of life !
Flawlessness is external while
Flaw lies within, We are made of love.

ARCHANA BHARATHI

Will you be there
till I make it to you?

The dark nights that
both of us enduring
will run out someday!

You have me by your side
To see through the dark;
To fight with the nights;
To love the waiting --
Till i make it to you

Walking through the storms
just to reach your arms,
My dispirited heart flames up
just by thinking of your face...

The longing to be yours
is killing me slowly...
All the paths lead to you,
All these times show you,
All of me is reflecting YOU.

Will you be there
till I make it to you?

ARCHANA BHARATHI

From darkness to You

My eyes keep searching
for you in each and
every room of house
with a flickering candle…

The serene night for all
is not the same for me-
My quest for your face
is guarding the flame
of the dying candle…

The last room is there
but where are the keys?
Have I lost them?
Do you believe that
as I lost it?
Or am I hopeless
to open the door?

ARCHANA BHARATHI

Before the last flame,
My trembling hands and
The dreadful heart
Finally dared to unlock!

In the darkness
I found my light
In the dusty room
I found my treasure
My home is You…

What could you
Give me more than
This peace and Love?

ARCHANA BHARATHI

Never away

As the bravery
To face the sword,
I choose to
Me before You
And always
You before me…

We thought
we're unarmed
unless we realized
moving a step away
from each other…
Don't drive me
to the misery
with your words,
The long road
to reach you
is neither smooth
nor mapped…

ARCHANA BHARATHI

Did I say it
Your words?
How can I say
it mine or yours
when we have
Become 'us'?

When every time
You bleed
because of me.
I want us
One step closer
and not away!

Till ever it is
ME BEFORE YOU
& YOU BEFORE ME
With love!

ARCHANA BHARATHI

My Asylum

Who can I be true to
in the tussle of life
when the arrows are
thrown to spoil peace?

Who can I be true to
when the world
reminds me that
misunderstanding
is the only finale
if I let the veil down?

While walking with
the uncertainties
in the dark field,
The wind unfurls
to remove the mask
in an asylum where
the voice of my
inner self is tolerated...

ARCHANA BHARATHI

The ripped soul
finds it comfort
in the silence of
the safest place...
The home to be
the Truest self

Who can I be true to
when I find a home
to be the Truest
It is all the strength
I ever wanted -
My asylum!
My home!

ARCHANA BHARATHI

The world of us

Let us not forget
that we are still
two little kids
dressed up as
Adults…
I'm reminding
this to you
because I need
Your heart and soul
to stay young
And to revive
the tired soul…
To make you trust
that here is a
World of ours
To just be YOU.

ARCHANA BHARATHI

Guiding light

To seal the love
with the rays of
Sunshine reflecting
in your eyes-
I find my way out
from the lost woods
fearlessly removing
the blindfold of life.
You make me fearless…

ARCHANA BHARATHI

A Love beyond time

To hold your face
in my eyes
at my last breathe
is all my privilege.

To freeze your name
in my lips
at my memory slip
is all my tribute.

To feel your presence
near to me
at my eternal rest
is all my indebtedness.

How could I leave you
when the last beat
refuses to stop
just to be with you
A little longer?

ARCHANA BHARATHI

How could I ever
be alive if not
Your eyes,
Your smiles,
And You around me...

Would you let me go?
Without the privilege
I asked for,
Without the tribute
I pay for you,
Without clearing
the indebtedness
I owe to you,
Would you let me go?

Drowning in you

How could I build a dam,
when each and
every drop of me
is striving to show you
the ocean of love!?

ARCHANA BHARATHI

You are the fuel to my hibernated heart.

Love never disappears. Whether it is accepted or rejected, it stays—floating in the air, unseen but always there. Longing, grief, and love are all the same in different forms. If you have longed for someone, if your heart has ached, if you have felt warmth in a quiet moment—know that it was love.

For so many reasons—because of time, distance, the weight of the world, or simply because someone could not reciprocate, accept, or choose your love—people have been separated. But love does not end with separation. The love I feel, the love you feel, the love we have all given—it stays in the air for millions of years. Somewhere, somehow, it still exists. It finds a way, in a stranger's smile, in the rustling of leaves, in the warmth of the sun touching your skin.

If your love was lost, know that it was not in vain. It is still alive in this world, even if you cannot see it.

Thank you for choosing this book, for spending time with my words. You welcomed my thoughts into your world, and for that, I am grateful.

I love you.

Always,

AB

About the Author

AB is a poet finding beauty in life, love, and hope. She believes that love—whether shared with parents, siblings, friends, or even strangers—makes life meaningful. A staunch believer in the power of emotions, she sees human nature as a canvas painted with gestures, efforts, and words that express love in its purest form.

The Scent of Forgotten Love is her first poetry book.

Writing in a way that many can connect with, she captures the essence of life, memories and the quiet moments that shape human connections. A wild heart and a free spirit, she weaves emotions into verses that drift through the soul. *The Scent of Forgotten Love* offers readers a journey through love, loss, and the warmth of love that never goes away—the enduring power of hope.

You can visit her on Instagram @archana_bharathi_